W9-CLI-795

DISCARD

SUPERMARKET

by Kathleen Krull

12/01 B+T

DISCARD

illustrated by

Melanie Hope Greenberg

J
381
K

Holiday House / New York

To my partner-in-groceries, Paul
K. K.

To Key Food, Brooklyn Heights, New York,
and a melange of thanks to:
Donald, Enrico, Israel and Ivan,
Anna "Arugula" Kelly, Barbara "Chef-Girl-Ardee" Yvinne,
Darlene, Fred, George, Joan, Joyce, Julia, Martin,
Modesta, Muhammed, Omar, and Ruth
M. H. G.

Text copyright © 2001 by Kathleen Krull
Illustrations copyright © 2001 by Melanie Hope Greenberg
All Rights Reserved
Printed in the United States of America
The text typeface is Barcelona.
The medium of the artwork is gouache.
www.holidayhouse.com
First Edition

Library of Congress Cataloging-in-Publication Data
Krull, Kathleen.
Supermarket / by Kathleen Krull;
illustrated by Melanie Hope Greenberg.
p. cm.
Summary: Explains modern supermarkets and how they work,
discussing how they organize, display, and keep track
of the items they sell.
ISBN 0-8234-1546-5
1. Supermarkets—Juvenile literature.
2. Supermarkets—United States—Juvenile literature.
[1. Supermarkets.] I. Greenberg, Melanie Hope, ill. II Title.
HF5469.K76 2001

381'.148'0973—dc21
99-088042

Shopping carts clang.

Magic doors whiz open and shut.
Colors glow under bright white lights.
So many breakfasts, lunches, and dinners!
It's all at a special, necessary, very real place:
the supermarket.

The supermarket is a whole world of its own. Where does all this crunchy, munchy, sweet, sour, fiery, frozen, fabulous food come from?
ON SALE
SPECIALS
The doors don't really open by magic. When an electric "eye" overhead "sees" you coming, it starts a motor to open the doors.
GOURMET FOODS
sugar/salt/ cake mix
JUICE & SODA

OATS & MORE
According to surveys, shoppers decide in their first 8 seconds whether they feel comfortable in a store. The first thing they see helps them decide.
milk
milk
milk
milk
milk
APER GOODS
CEREAL

It all begins on farms.
Our food comes from places with lots of sunshine, rich soil, and clean water.
Farmers make decisions every day during the long months of growing.

At harvesttime, workers pick the fruits and vegetables. They pack everything neatly in boxes and load the boxes onto trucks.

Small trucks, big trucks, gigantic trucks—
all rev up their engines.
Every night, drivers take off from farms or warehouses.
They zoom down the highway toward your town.

Among many other foods, American Indians introduced to the rest of the world chocolate, potatoes, tomatoes, beans, peppers, and, most important, corn. Some form of corn appears in more supermarket foods today than probably anything else.

In early America, most people were farmers. American Indians taught the new arrivals what to grow.

Families grew all their own food.
Later, they traded food with one another
to get other things they needed.
They started using money to buy things
at town marketplaces.
Soon there were general stores
where you could buy almost anything...

and little, family-run grocery stores—"mom-and-pop" stores. Stores became bigger, dividing items into different departments.

The supermarket is an American invention. In 1859, the Great Atlantic and Pacific Tea Company opened one of the first supermarket chains: the A&P.

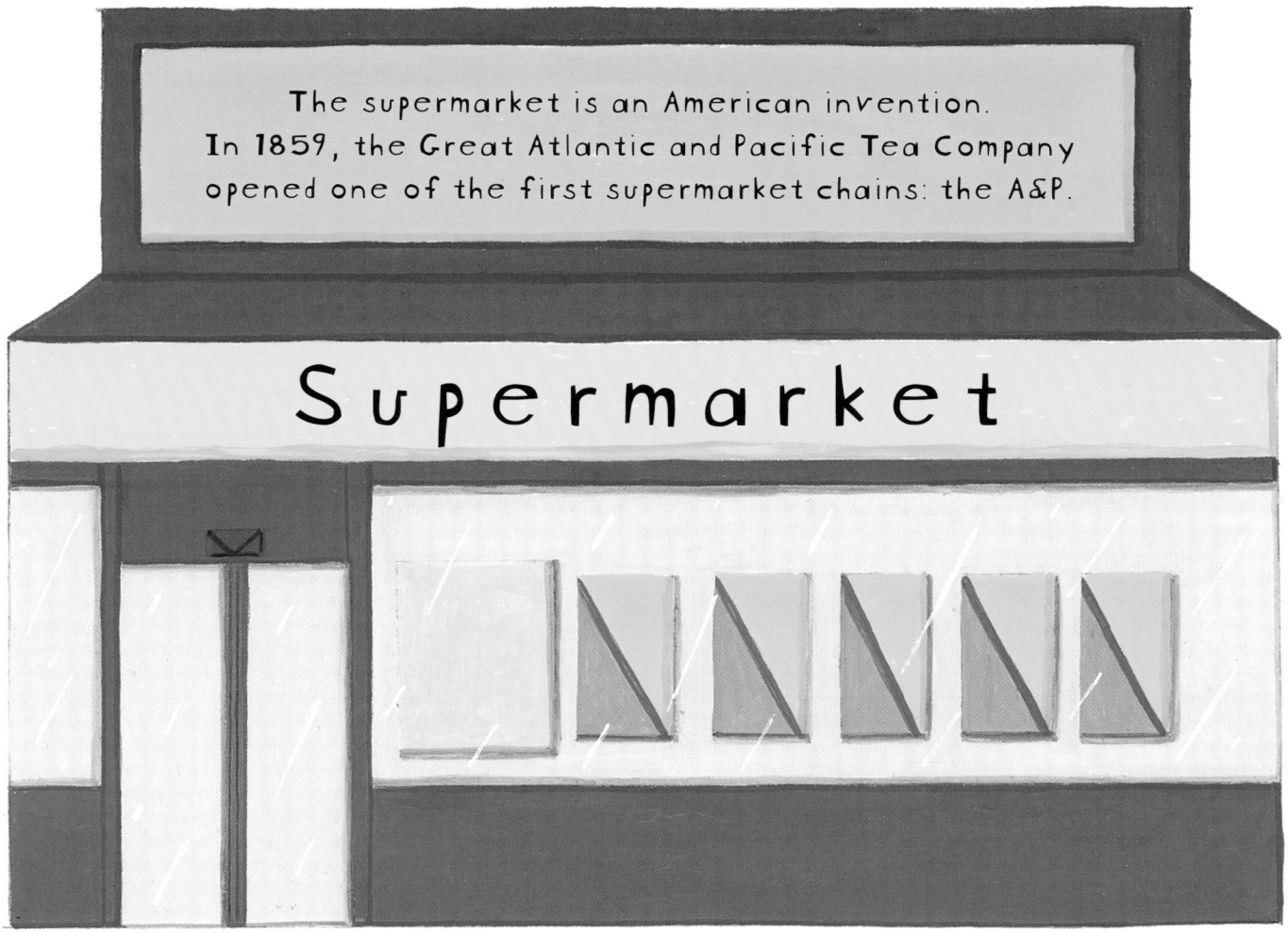

Now we have an amazing place where every morning workers have a whole "super" market all ready for you. They have unpacked thousands of boxes and arranged everything on the shelves, just so.

THE FOOD PYRAMID

Some kids might think of the supermarket
as the place that sells candy.
But sweets are just a small part of what we eat.

You can find more variety in the fruit and vegetable section than anywhere else: fresh, juicy, strange, familiar.

Shoppers look, touch, sniff, compare, weigh—
and watch out for automatic sprayers.

Beds of crushed ice keep the meats and fish fresh. Butchers cut or grind meat into different sizes and wrap packages in plastic.

For most of human history, food has often spoiled before it could be eaten. Not until the 1800s did people learn how to preserve food by sealing it inside metal cans. Around 1830, the English figured out a way to chill their food with machines.

The best smells float around the bakery. Bakers sometimes bake thousands of doughnuts a day and at least a dozen different kinds of bread.

Just about everyone stops in the dairy section. Behind all the eggs, milk, yogurt, and cheese is a refrigerated area keeping everything cold.

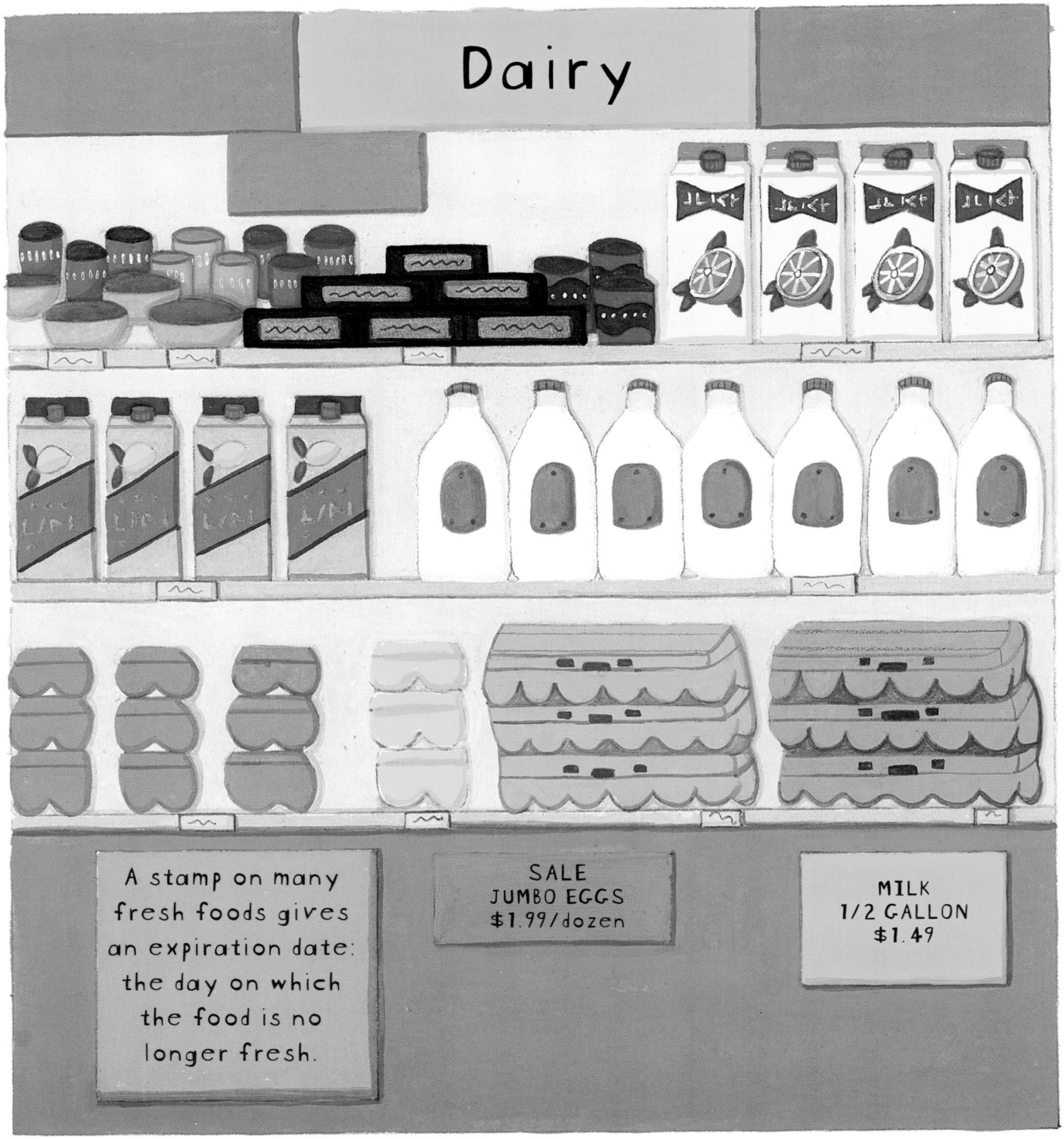

A sweater is handy in the frozen foods section, where the air is coldest. Zippy music makes some people hum along or dance right in the aisle.

The store is packed with cereal, soups, spices, and even "nonfoods."

At the checkout counter, people try to pick the shortest line. An electronic scanner "reads" the bar codes on most products and prints out the prices. A cash register adds up the cost of your food. Baggers ask "Paper or plastic?" and pack up your groceries.

Think about all the people who move food from the farms to your kitchen shelves!

Even more goes on behind the scenes.
Managers keep track of inventory, their supply of foods.
Using computers, they find out what is selling
and order more for the trucks to deliver.

There are stockrooms with food ready to be moved
onto empty shelves; bathrooms for the workers;
a room where they eat their lunch;

a place for garbage, damaged products, and spoiled food; a place where boxes get unloaded;

and a place where empty boxes get recycled.

And cleaning supplies.
No one wants to see a hint of dirt or germs at the supermarket.

The supermarket has row after row of colors, shapes, and words that shout. Some kids learn how to read right here, from signs, labels, and shopping lists. The supermarket is a good place to practice math, too.

Americans spend more than $440 BILLION a year at our supermarkets.
4 oz. $1.99
5 oz. $2.49
COUPON SPECIAL
NEW
COUPON SPECIAL
SALE
3 gallons for $4.99
MANAGER'S SPECIAL
Over half of shoppers, especially women, use a shopping list to make sure they don't forget anything. The average shopping list contains 22 items. Still, over half of what shoppers buy in a store is not on their list.
ENJOY
16 oz. $1.79

A supermarket helps us celebrate holidays and big moments in our lives.

The supermarket even helps us know who we are. Are we the kind of person who likes macaroni and cheese in a box?
Or spaghetti in a can? Orange juice or grape juice? Peanut butter: smooth or crunchy? Definitely pizza, but what kind?

Shopping for groceries is a super family time,
deciding which things to pile in your cart.

Every family has to go—week in, week out.
The supermarket helps to shape the lives of everyone.

The supermarket is never quite the same from day to day. New items are added all the time, especially from around the world. Some markets have other stores right inside—worlds of their own.

VIDEO VILLA
Pasta & More
SALAD BAR
Bob's Blossoms

Supermarkets are always changing.
Now some people order groceries
right on the Internet,
without even leaving the house.
But the supermarket will always be around—
one place that is never boring,
a very real place like nowhere else.

J
381
K

Krull, Kathleen.

Supermarket.

DISCARD

Hiram Halle Memorial Library
Pound Ridge, New York